GRADE

eVeryday Comprehension
Intervention Activities

Table of Contents

Using Everyday Comprehension Intervention Activities

Reading with full text comprehension is the ultimate goal of all reading instruction. Students who read the words but don't comprehend them aren't really reading at all. Research has shown that explicit comprehension strategy instruction helps students understand and remember what they read, which allows them to communicate what they've learned with others and perform better in testing situations.

Although some students master comprehension strategies easily during regular classroom instruction, many others need additional re-teaching opportunities to master these essential strategies. The Everyday Intervention Activities series provides easy-to-use, five-day intervention units for Grades K–5. These units are structured around a research-based Model-Guide-Practice-Apply approach. You can use these activities in a variety of intervention models, including Response to Intervention (RTI).

Standards-Based Comprehension Strategies in Everyday Intervention Activities

Comprehension Strategy	Strategy Definition	K
Make Predictions	Determine what might happen next in a story or nonfiction piece. Predictions are based on information presented in the text.	✔
Identify Sequence of Events	Determine the order of events for topics such as history, science, or biography. Determine the steps to make or do something.	✔
Analyze Story Elements	Analyze the setting and plot (problem/solution) in a fiction text.	✔
Analyze Character	Analyze story characters based on information and on clues and evidence in the text, including description, actions, dialogue, feelings, and traits.	✔
Identify Main Idea and Supporting Details	Determine what the paragraph, page, or chapter is mostly about. Sometimes the main idea is stated and sometimes it is implied. Students must choose details that support the main idea, not "just any detail."	✔
Summarize	Take key ideas from the text and put them together to create a shorter version of the original text. Summaries should have few, if any, details.	✔
Compare and Contrast	Find ways that two things are alike and different.	✔
Identify Cause and Effect	Find things that happened (effect) and why they happened (cause). Text may contain multiple causes and effects.	✔
Make Inferences	Determine what the author is suggesting without directly stating it. Inferences are usually made during reading and are made from one or two pieces of information from the text. Students' inferences will vary but must be made from the evidence in the text and background knowledge.	✔

Getting Started

In just five simple steps, Everyday Comprehension Intervention Activities provides everything you need to identify students' comprehension needs and to provide targeted, research-based intervention.

1. PRE-ASSESS to identify students' comprehension needs.
Use the pre-assessment to identify the strategies your students need to master.

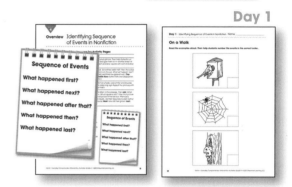

2. MODEL the strategy.
Every five-day unit targets a specific strategy. On Day 1, use the teacher prompts and reproducible activity to introduce and model the strategy.

Day 1

3. GUIDE PRACTICE and APPLY.
Use the reproducible practice activities for Days 2, 3, and 4 to build students' understanding of, and proficiency with, the strategy.

Day 2

Day 3

Day 4

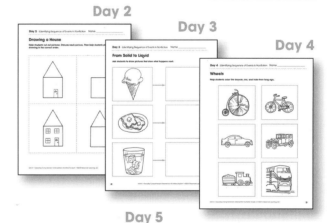

4. MONITOR progress.
Administer the Day 5 reproducible assessment to monitor each student's progress and to make instructional decisions.

Day 5

5. POST-ASSESS to document student progress.
Use the post-assessment to measure students' progress as a result of your interventions.

Using Everyday Intervention for RTI

According to the National Center on Response to Intervention, RTI "integrates assessment and intervention within a multi-level prevention system to maximize student achievement and to reduce behavior problems." This model of instruction and assessment allows schools to identify at-risk students, monitor their progress, provide research-proven interventions, and "adjust the intensity and nature of those interventions depending on a student's responsiveness."

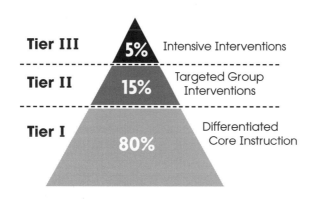

RTI models vary from district to district, but the most prevalent model is a three-tiered approach to instruction and assessment.

The Three Tiers of RTI	Using Everyday Intervention Activities
Tier I: Differentiated Core Instruction • Designed for all students • Preventive, proactive, standards-aligned instruction • Whole- and small-group differentiated instruction • Ninety-minute, daily core reading instruction in the five essential skill areas: phonics, phonemic awareness, comprehension, vocabulary, fluency	• Use whole-group comprehension mini-lessons to introduce and guide practice with comprehension strategies that all students need to learn. • Use any or all of the units in the order that supports your core instructional program.
Tier II: Targeted Group Interventions • For at-risk students • Provide thirty minutes of daily instruction beyond the ninety-minute Tier I core reading instruction • Instruction is conducted in small groups of three to five students with similar needs	• Select units based on your students' areas of need (the pre-assessment can help you identify these). • Use the units as week-long, small-group mini-lessons.
Tier III: Intensive Interventions • For high-risk students experiencing considerable difficulty in reading • Provide up to sixty minutes of additional intensive intervention each day in addition to the ninety-minute Tier I core reading instruction • More intense and explicit instruction • Instruction conducted individually or with smaller groups of one to three students with similar needs	• Select units based on your students' areas of need. • Use the units as one component of an intensive comprehension intervention program.

Overview Making Predictions in Fiction

Directions and Sample Answers for Activity Pages

Day 1	See "Provide a Real-World Example" below.
Day 2	Read and discuss the book cover and the clues it provides. Then discuss the pictures. Help students color the pictures they predict will be in a book about a king's birthday. (birthday card, cake, balloons, queen)
Day 3	Read and discuss the book cover and the clues it provides. **Say:** *Ari is going to paint a picture for Show and Tell. What do you predict will happen?* Discuss students' predictions, and then ask them to draw a prediction in the box. **Say:** *Mya is going to sing a song for Show and Tell. What do you predict will happen?* Discuss students' predictions, and then ask them to draw a prediction in the box. (Responses will vary.)
Day 4	Read and discuss each book cover and the clues it provides. Discuss the clues in each picture. Then help students predict which pictures will be in each book and draw a line to those pictures. (**Bob's Book of B:** ball, banana, bear. **Tia's Tale of T:** table, tiger, tent.)
Day 5	Ask students to listen to the story. **Ask:** *Where do you predict the mice will move? Color the picture that shows your prediction.* Afterward, meet individually with students to discuss their results. Use their responses to plan further instruction and review. (to the circus)

Provide a Real-World Example

◆ Hand out the Day 1 activity page.

◆ **Say:** *My friend is going someplace fun next Saturday. He will buy a ticket. He will look at lots of animals. He will go to the gift shop before he goes home.*

◆ Ask students to look at the pictures. **Say:** *A ticket, animals, and a gift shop are clues. You can use the clues to predict—or make a good guess about— where my friend plans to go. Where do you predict he will go?*

◆ Discuss that all of the places fit at least one of the clues, but only the zoo has tickets, animals, and a gift shop. Ask students to color the picture of the zoo. Then explain that we can also make predictions about stories we listen to. Write the following on chart paper:

Making Predictions

Think about the clues.

Think about what might happen.

Name _____

Saturday Fun

Look at each picture. Then help students predict where the friend will go if he or she buys a ticket, sees animals, and visits a gift shop.

MALL

MOVIES

Now Showing

ZOO

PETS

The King's Birthday

Read and discuss the book cover. Ask students to color the pictures they predict will be in the book.

Name _____

Show and Tell

Read and discuss the book cover. Ask students to look at each page and draw what they predict will happen next.

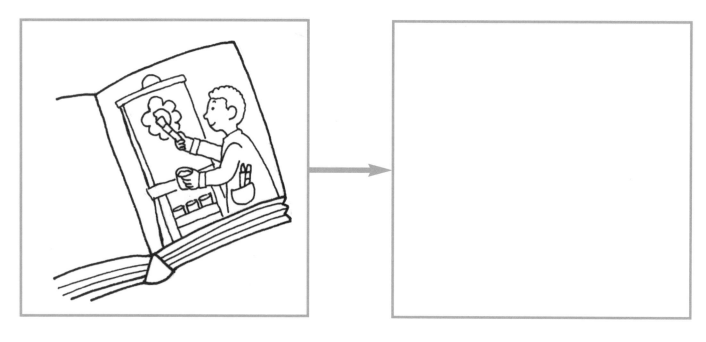

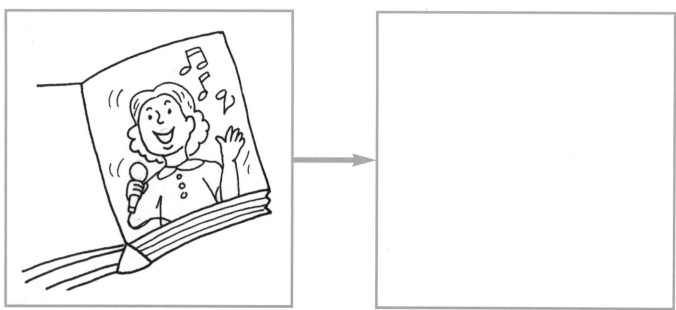

Letter Books

Read and discuss each book cover. Help students predict which items they will find in each book. Ask them to draw a line connecting each item with that book.

Assessment

**Read the passage aloud to students. Ask students to predict where the mice will move.
Ask students to color the picture that shows their prediction.**

"I have an idea," said Marty Mouse.

"What is it?" asked Mae and Moe.

"Let's move to a new home," said Marty.
"I found one that has lots of other animals.
It has lots of food, too. People even drop
popcorn and peanuts on the ground!"

"That sounds like FUN!" said Mae and Moe. "Let's go!"

Overview Making Predictions in Nonfiction

Directions and Sample Answers for Activity Pages

Day 1	See "Provide a Real-World Example" below.
Day 2	Read and discuss the book cover and the evidence it provides. Then discuss the pictures. Help students color the pictures they predict will be in a book about how to play baseball. (cap, bat, baseball, mitt)
Day 3	Read and discuss the sign and the evidence it provides. **Say:** *Many parks have signs. This park just put up a new sign. What do you predict people will do when they see the sign?* Discuss students' predictions, and then ask them to draw a prediction in the box. **Say:** *What do you predict animals will do when they see the sign?* Discuss students' predictions, and then ask them to draw a prediction in the box. (People will likely read the sign and stay on the sidewalk. Animals can't read, so they'll likely walk on the grass.)
Day 4	Read and discuss each advertisement and the evidence it provides. Discuss the evidence in each picture. Then help students predict which people will call about the kittens and which people will call about the car and draw a line to those people. (**Kittens:** man with cats; mom and daughter in car. **Car:** woman walking dogs; chef riding bike to work.)
Day 5	Ask students to listen to the instructions. **Ask:** *What do you predict the cabin will look like? Color the picture that shows your prediction.* Afterward, meet individually with students to discuss their results. Use their responses to plan further instruction and review. (third picture)

Provide a Real-World Example

◆ Hand out the Day 1 activity page.

◆ **Say:** *Think about things we often use at school. Tell a partner two things we often use at school.*

◆ Ask students to look at the pictures. **Say:** *The things we often use at school are evidence. You can use the evidence to predict—or make a good guess—what we will use at school tomorrow. What do you predict we will use?*

◆ Ask students to color the pictures that show their predictions. Accept any responses for which students can provide evidence. Then explain that we can also make predictions about things we learn about the world. Write the following on chart paper:

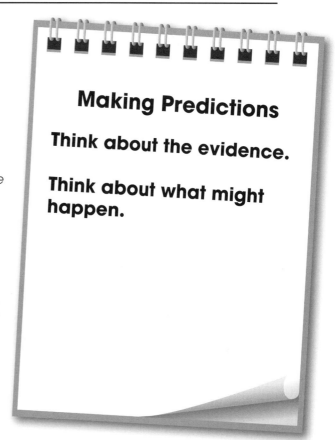

Making Predictions

Think about the evidence.

Think about what might happen.

Tomorrow at School

Ask students to make predictions about what they are likely to use at school tomorrow.

How to Play Baseball

Read and discuss the book cover. Then help students predict which pictures will be in the book.

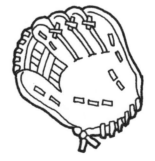

Park Signs

Read and discuss the sign. Ask students to look at each picture.
Then ask students to draw what they predict will happen next.

For Sale

Read and discuss each advertisement. Help students predict who will answer each advertisement. Ask students to draw a line connecting their predictions to each advertisement.

Assessment

Read the passage aloud to students. Ask students to predict what the cabin will look like. Ask students to color the picture that shows their prediction.

You can make a cabin out of pretzel sticks.

Cut a door and window out of a square box.

Glue a cardboard roof on the box.

Glue pretzel sticks in straight rows across the box and roof.

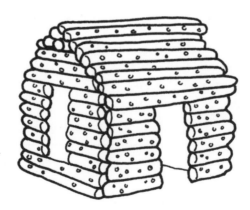

Overview Identifying Sequence of Events in Fiction

Directions and Sample Answers for Activity Pages

Day 1	See "Provide a Real-World Example" below.
Day 2	**Say:** *Ron spent most of the day in his room.* Discuss each picture. Then help students cut out the pictures, put them in the correct order, and glue them on to another sheet of paper. (waking up, cleaning room, playing game with friend, going to bed)
Day 3	**Say:** *Eva has fun at school. Look at the first picture. What is Eva doing? What could Eva do next? Draw a picture to show something Eva could do next.* Repeat with the second and third rows. (**Top Row:** listen to a story; use a computer; or check out a book. **Middle Row:** finger paint or paint at an easel. **Bottom Row:** build something with the blocks.)
Day 4	**Say:** *Joy is getting ready to eat dinner. Look at the two pictures of Joy. Color the picture that shows what Joy does first.* (wash her hands) *Ben and Vic are getting ready to go to the store with Dad. Color the picture that shows what Ben and Vic do first.* (run to the car) *Todd and Tess are getting ready to swim. Color the picture that shows what Todd and Tess do first.* (get the pool)
Day 5	Help students cut out the pictures. Ask them to listen to the story. Then **ask:** *What did Lou and his brother do first? Glue that picture in the first box. What did they do next? Glue that picture in the next box. What did they do last? Glue that picture in the last box.* Afterward, meet individually with students to discuss their results. Use their responses to plan further instruction and review. (**First:** played basketball. **Next:** ate pizza. **Last:** went to the playground.)

Provide a Real-World Example

◆ Hand out the Day 1 activity page.

◆ **Say:** *Once I was hungry for a snack. First, I found a banana to eat. Then I found some carrots to eat. Finally, I found some crackers to eat. I ate the foods in a certain order, or sequence.*

◆ Remind students that the first thing you ate was a banana. Write **1** on the board. Ask students to locate the banana on their page and write **1** in the box. Repeat the process with the carrots (**2**) and crackers (**3**).

◆ Explain that we can also think about the order things happen in stories. Name a simple story you have read to the class, and ask students to help you recall the events in order. Then write the following on chart paper:

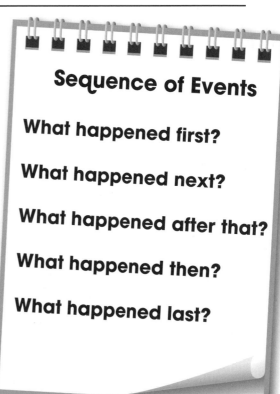

Sequence of Events

What happened first?

What happened next?

What happened after that?

What happened then?

What happened last?

Snack Time

Read the order aloud. Then help students number the boxes to show the correct order.

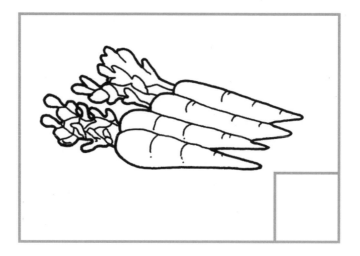

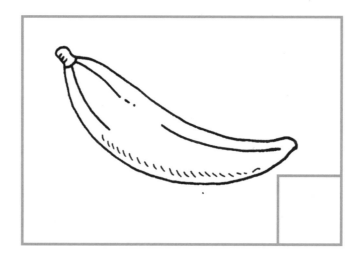

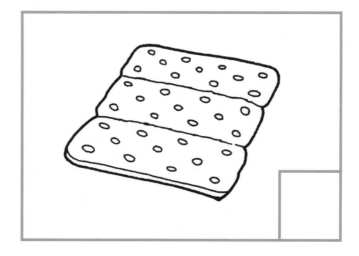

Ron's Room

Discuss each picture. Help students cut out each picture.
Then ask them to paste the pictures on to another sheet of paper in the correct order.

Fun at School

Discuss each picture. Then ask students to draw what Eva might do *next*.

Getting Ready

Discuss the pictures in each row. Ask students to color the picture that shows what happened *first*.

Assessment

Read the passage aloud to students. Then ask students to cut and paste the pictures in the correct order.

"I had a fun day with my big brother," said Lou.

"What did you do?" asked Sky.

"First, we played basketball. Then we had pizza. Before we came home, we went to the playground," said Lou.

"That IS a fun day," said Sky. "I wish I had a big brother!"

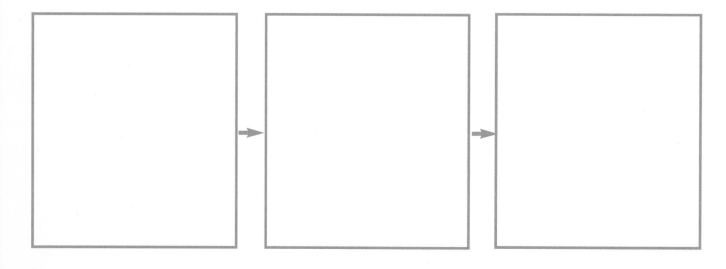

Overview Identifying Sequence of Events in Nonfiction

Directions and Sample Answers for Activity Pages

Day 1	See "Provide a Real-World Example" below.
Day 2	**Say:** *Some people like to draw houses.* Discuss each picture. Then help students cut out the pictures, put them in the correct order, and glue them on to another sheet of paper. (square; square with roof; square with roof and door; square with roof and door and windows)
Day 3	**Say:** *Ice cream, butter, and ice cubes are solids. Sometimes solids melt. Then the solids are liquids. Look at the ice cream. The ice cream is in the sun. What will happen next?* Repeat with the second row (butter on hot toast) and third row (glass of ice). (**Top Row:** ice cream melts and drips from cone. **Middle Row:** butter melts and disappears into toast. **Bottom Row:** ice cubes turn to water.)
Day 4	**Say:** *We go many places on wheels. A bicycle has wheels. Look at the two bicycles. Color the picture that shows a bicycle people rode long ago.* Repeat the process with the car and train. (first bicycle, second car, first train)
Day 5	Help students cut out the pictures. Ask them to listen to the passage. Then **ask:** *What happens first? Glue that picture in the first box. What happens next? Glue that picture in the next box. Then what happens? Glue that picture in the last box.* Afterward, meet individually with students to discuss their results. Use their responses to plan further instruction and review. (**First:** acorn sits on ground. **Next:** new oak tree grows. **Last:** acorns grow on the tree.)

Provide a Real-World Example

◆ Hand out the Day 1 activity page.

◆ **Say:** *Once I went for a walk. I saw many animal homes. First, I saw a spider on a web. Then I saw a squirrel peeking out of a hole in a tree. Finally, I saw a bird at its birdhouse. I saw the animals in a certain order, or sequence.*

◆ Remind students that the first thing you saw was a spider on a web. Write **1** on the board. Ask students to locate the spider on their page and write **1** in the box. Repeat the process with the squirrel (**2**) and bird (**3**).

◆ Explain that we can also think about the order things happen as we learn about the world. Then write the following on chart paper:

Sequence of Events

What happened first?

What happened next?

What happened after that?

What happened then?

What happened last?

On a Walk

Read the examples aloud. Then help students number the events in the correct order.

Drawing a House

Help students cut out pictures. Discuss each picture. Then help students place each drawing in the correct order.

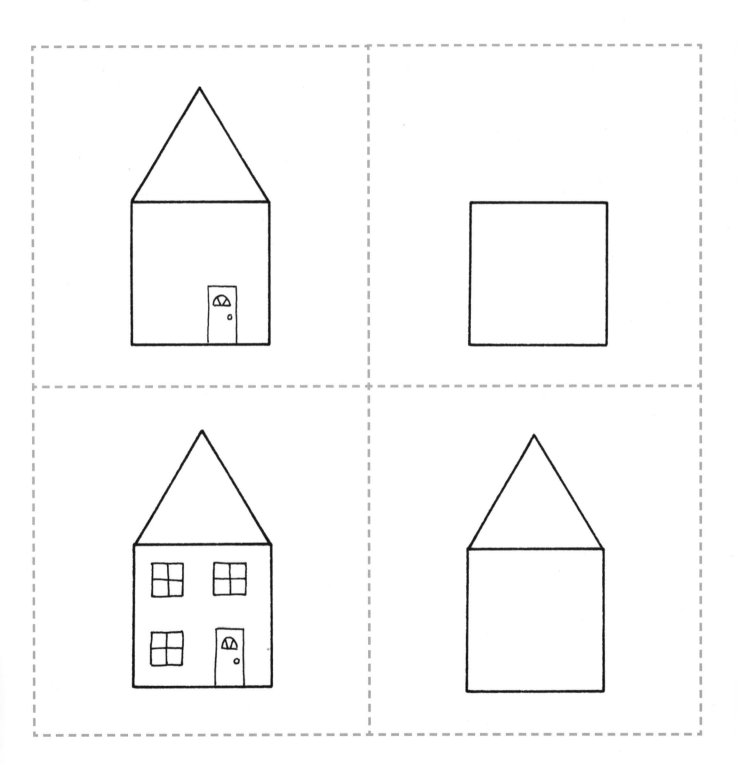

From Solid to Liquid

Ask students to draw pictures that show what happens next.

Wheels

Help students color the bicycle, car, and train from long ago.

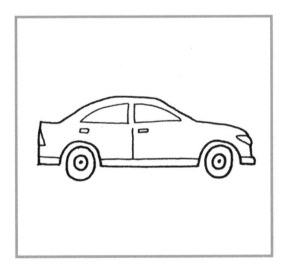

Assessment

Read the passage aloud. Then ask what happens first, next, and last.

Have you ever seen an acorn?

Did you know an acorn grows into an oak tree?

First, the acorn is on the ground.

Next, the acorn grows into a tree.

Then, new acorns grow on the tree.

The new acorns fall to the ground.

They grow into new trees!

Overview Analyzing Story Elements: Setting

Directions and Sample Answers for Activity Pages

Day 1	See "Provide a Real-World Example" below.
Day 2	Discuss each picture. Then help students color each picture that shows a setting where a story could take place. (barn, room, pond)
Day 3	Remind students that seasons can be a part of setting. Ask them to point to each picture in the right column as you name the season. Then discuss the pictures in the left column. **Say:** *Each picture tells a story. Draw a line to the season the story might take place in.* Assist as needed. (**Picking Apples:** Fall. **Swimming:** Summer. **Flying a Kite:** Spring. **Sitting by the Fireplace:** Winter.)
Day 4	Remind students that places are a part of setting. Discuss places students went to yesterday. Talk about places they have been to and might go to today. Predict places they might go tomorrow. Then help students draw their ideas in the labeled boxes. (Responses will vary.)
Day 5	Ask students to listen to the story. Then **ask:** *Where does the story take place? Color the picture on the top row. When does the story take place? Color the picture on the bottom row.* Afterward, meet individually with students to discuss their results. Use their responses to plan further instruction and review. (in a library, daytime)

Provide a Real-World Example

◆ Hand out the Day 1 activity page.

◆ **Say:** *Our school is a setting, or place. We will take a walk around our school.*

◆ Take students on a brief walk through the halls. Point out items that are typical in a school, such as bulletin boards, a water fountain, an office, and a gym. When you return to the classroom, ask students to draw three things they saw. Invite them to share their drawings with the class.

◆ **Say:** *A place is one part of a setting. Another part of a setting is time. Do we come to school at night or during the day? Color the picture that shows the time we come to school.*

◆ Explain that we can also think about places and times in stories. Name some stories you have read to the class. Ask students to think of words that describe the places and times. Write their ideas on chart paper:

Places

school
home
park
forest
castle
soccer field
ocean

Times

day
night
summer
winter
spring
fall
long ago

Name _____

Around Our School

Ask students to draw these things they saw on their walk around school. Then ask them to color in the picture that shows the time of day we come to school.

Places

Discuss each picture. Then help students color the setting where a story could take place.

Seasons

Point to each season and read it aloud. Then ask students to draw a line to the season when the story might take place.

Spring

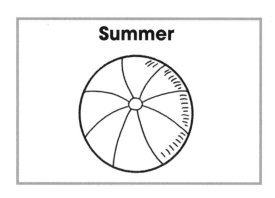

Summer

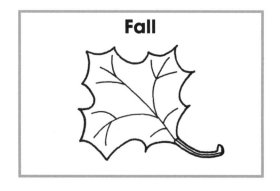

Fall

Winter

Yesterday, Today, and Tomorrow

Discuss places students went yesterday and today, and predict where they might go tomorrow. Then help students draw responses in each box.

Yesterday	**Today**	**Tomorrow**

Assessment

Read the story aloud. Then ask students to color where and when the story takes place.

"I love to come here," said Meg.

"Me, too!" said Rob.

"I am reading about a rocket ship," said Meg.

"Me, too!" said Rob.

"We must go!" said Mom. "It is almost time for lunch!"

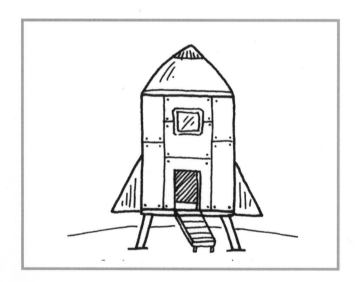

Overview Analyzing Story Elements: Plot

Directions and Sample Answers for Activity Pages

Day 1	See "Provide a Real-World Example" below.
Day 2	Discuss each picture. Then help students color the pictures that show a problem that could be in a story. (ambulance, angry boy, lion chasing monkey)
Day 3	**Say:** *Gigi wants a certain book to read, but she can't reach it.* Discuss the beginning and end of the story. Then help students draw what could happen in the middle. (Responses will vary.)
Day 4	**Say:** *Herman the hermit crab lived in a shell. One day, he grew too large for his shell.* Discuss the beginning and middle of the story. Then help students color the best ending. (Herman moved into a larger shell.)
Day 5	Help students cut out the pictures. Ask them to listen to the story. Then **ask:** *What happened at the beginning of the story? Glue that picture in the first box. What happened in the middle of the story? Glue that picture in the middle box. What happened at the end of the story? Glue that picture in the last box.* Afterward, meet individually with students to discuss their results. Use their responses to plan further instruction and review. (**Beginning:** boy talks to dad. **Middle:** boy looks in refrigerator. **End:** boy and dad eat carrot sticks.)

Provide a Real-World Example

◆ Hand out the Day 1 activity page.

◆ Display a ripped piece of paper and a paper clip, stapler, and some tape. **Say:** *My paper ripped. I thought of three ways to fix it. I could use a paper clip, a stapler, or some tape.* Discuss which one would work best (tape), and use the tape to repair the paper.

◆ **Say:** *Fixing my paper is like a story. At the beginning, I had a problem. My paper ripped.* Write **Beginning** on the board and circle the **B**. Ask students to find the picture that shows the beginning of the story and put a **B** beside it. Repeat the process with the middle of the story (getting out a paper clip, stapler, and some tape) and the end of the story (taping the paper).

◆ Tell students that the parts of a story are called the plot. Name a story you have read to the class, and discuss what happened at the beginning, in the middle, and at the end. Write the following on chart paper:

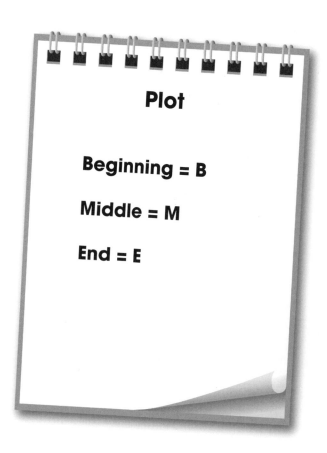

Plot

Beginning = B

Middle = M

End = E

Name _____

Rip!

Help students label each picture as the beginning, middle, or end (B, M, or E).

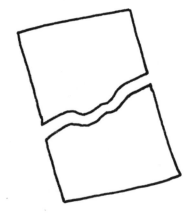

_____

_____

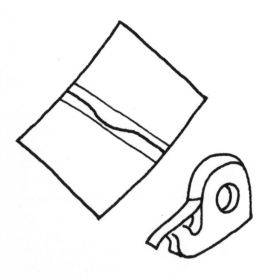

_____

Story Problems

Discuss each picture. Then help students color the pictures that show a problem.

Too High!

Discuss the beginning and end of the story depicted below. Then help students draw what might happen in the middle.

Beginning

Middle

End

Name _____

Herman

Read the story aloud. Then ask students to choose the end of the story.

Beginning

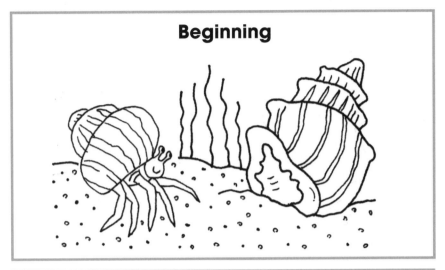

Middle

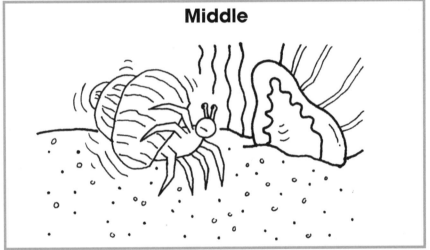

End

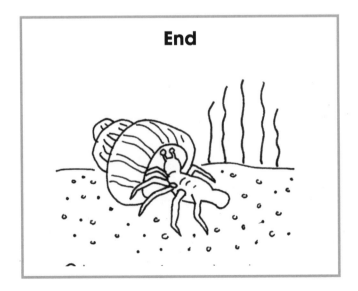

End

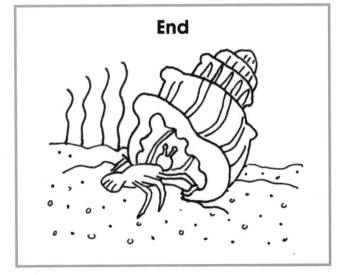

Assessment

Help students cut out the pictures. Read the story aloud to them. Then ask them to paste the pictures in the correct order.

"May I have a cracker?" asked Max.

"No," said Dad. "You may have a cracker after dinner, though."

"But I'm hungry now!" said Max.
He looked in the refrigerator.
"May I have some carrot sticks?" he asked.

"Yes!" said Dad. "I think I'll have some, too!"

Beginning	**Middle**	**End**

Overview Analyzing Character: Traits

Directions and Sample Answers for Activity Pages

Day 1	See "Provide a Real-World Example" below.
Day 2	Ask each student to draw a picture of a friend. Then ask them to think of a trait the friend has. Help them fill in the sentence to name the trait. Then invite students to share their drawings and sentences with the class. (Responses will vary.)
Day 3	Discuss what it means to be curious. Then talk about each picture. Ask students to circle **Yes** or **No** to show whether the cat in the picture is being curious. (**Yes:** looking under sofa, behind door, inside shoe, into cabinet. **No:** napping, eating.)
Day 4	Discuss what it means to be messy or neat. Help students cut out the pictures at the bottom of the page. Ask students to point to the words as you read the story aloud. Then help them glue the pictures in the correct boxes. (read in Ned's room, jump on the bed in May's.
Day 5	Help students cut out the pictures. Ask them to listen to the story. Then **ask:** *Which character is kind? Glue that character's picture in the top box. Which character is greedy? Glue that character's picture in the bottom box.* Afterward, meet individually with students to discuss their results. Use their responses to plan further instruction and review. (**Kind:** Ladybug. **Greedy:** Ant.)

Provide a Real-World Example

◆ Hand out the Day 1 activity page.

◆ **Say:** *Everyone looks different. Everyone acts differently, too. How someone acts is a trait. Some people are helpful. What does it mean to be helpful?*

◆ Allow time for students to discuss what it means to be helpful. Then **say:** *Find the picture of a girl who is being helpful. What is the girl doing?*

◆ Discuss how the girl is being helpful by picking up a pencil her friend dropped. Ask students to draw a circle around the picture of the girl being helpful. Then ask them to draw a picture of a time they were helpful. Invite students to share their drawings.

◆ Explain that we can also think about the ways characters in stories act. Name some characters in stories you have read to the class. Ask students to think of words that describe the characters. Write their ideas on chart paper:

Traits

helpful

lazy

funny

bossy

brave

shy

kind

mean

Being Helpful

Ask students: What does it mean to be helpful?

Tell students: Draw a picture of a time that you were helpful.

My Friend

Ask students to draw a friend. Help them complete the sentence below.

My friend is _____.

Curious Cat

Discuss what it means to be curious. Ask students: Do the pictures show the cat being curious? Then ask students to circle *yes* or *no* for each picture.

Yes   No

Yes   No

Yes   No

Yes   No

Yes   No

Yes   No

Messy May and Neat Ned

Read aloud. Ask students to cut and paste the pictures to complete each sentence.

This is May.

This is Ned.

May and Ned are friends.

May and Ned like to  in Ned's room.

May and Ned like to  in May's room!

Assessment

Read the story aloud. Then ask students to cut and paste the character next to the matching trait.

One day, Ladybug made a cake.

"Have some cake!" said Ladybug.

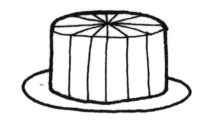

"Yum!" said Ant. Ant ate a piece of cake. Then he ate another piece. Then he ate another and another and another.

"I want more cake," said Ant.

"The cake is gone," said Ladybug.

"You could give me your piece," said Ant.

"Okay," said Ladybug. "But next time, I will eat my piece before you come!"

➔ **kind**

➔ **greedy**

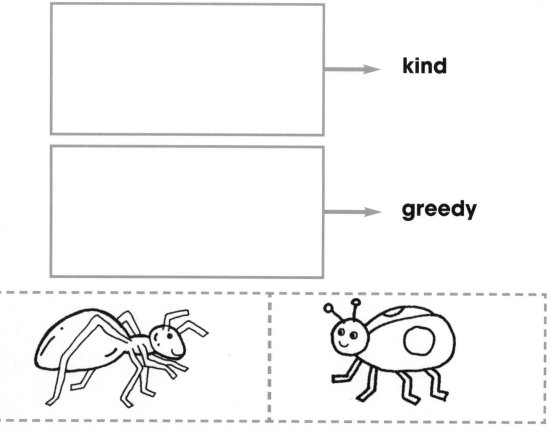

Overview   Analyzing Character: Feelings

Directions and Sample Answers for Activity Pages

Day 1	See "Provide a Real-World Example" below.
Day 2	Discuss the elephant's feelings in each picture. Then help students draw something that makes the elephant feel sad, mad, and glad. (Responses will vary.)
Day 3	Discuss what it means to feel surprised. Ask students to pretend the class is going on a walk around the neighborhood. Then help them circle **Yes** or **No** to show whether they would feel surprised to see each object, person, or animal on their walk. (Answers will vary.)
Day 4	Discuss what it means to feel tired. Help students cut out the pictures at the bottom of the page. Ask students to point to the words as you read the story aloud. Then help them glue the pictures in the correct boxes. (made the girls laugh; made the boys laugh; made the monkeys laugh; the clown feels tired)
Day 5	Help students cut out the pictures. Ask them to listen to the story. Then **ask:** Which character is lonely? Glue that character's picture in the top box. Which character is proud? Glue that character's picture in the bottom box. Afterward, meet individually with students to discuss their results. Use their responses to plan further instruction and review. (**Lonely:** Turtle. **Proud:** Frog.)

Provide a Real-World Example

◆ Hand out the Day 1 activity page.

◆ **Say:** *We have different feelings at different times. Sometimes we feel scared. Show me how your face looks when you feel scared. What is something that makes you feel scared?*

◆ Allow time for students to discuss feeling scared. Repeat the process with other feelings, such as feeling mad, excited, sad, and proud.

◆ **Say:** *A boy named Hal feels happy. Find the picture of Hal when he feels happy. Why is he happy?*

◆ Discuss that Hal feels happy because his friend came to visit. Ask students to draw a circle around the picture of happy Hal. Then ask them to draw a picture of a time they felt happy. Invite students to share their drawings.

◆ Explain that we can also think about the ways characters in stories feel. Name some characters in stories you have read to the class. Ask students to think of words that describe how the characters felt in different situations in the story. Write their ideas on chart paper.

Feelings

scared

mad

excited

sad

proud

happy

lonely

surprised

Name _____

Happy Hal

Ask students to circle the picture that shows Hal feeling happy.

Now ask students to draw a time when they were happy.

Sad, Mad, or Glad?

Discuss the elephant's feelings in each picture. Then ask students to draw something that makes the elephant feel sad, mad, and glad.

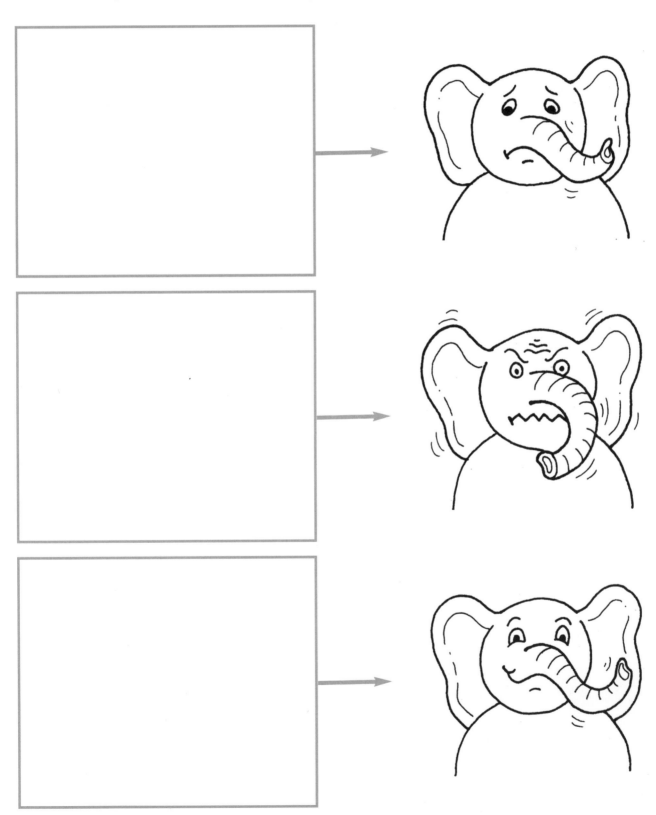

Surprise!

Discuss what it means to feel surprised. Then ask students to think about which of these pictures are surprises. Have them circle *yes* or *no* for each.

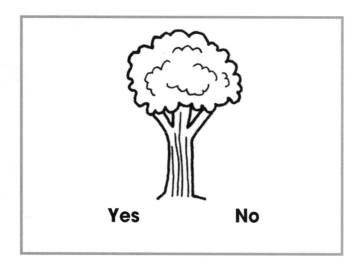

Yes   **No**

Yes   **No**

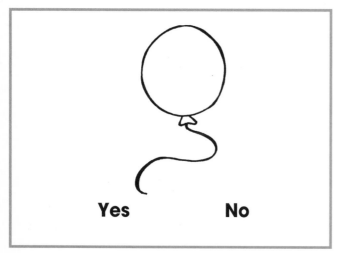

Yes   **No**

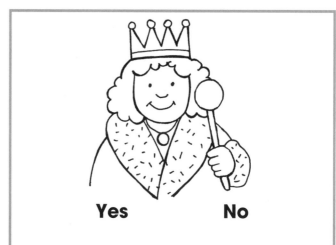

Yes   **No**

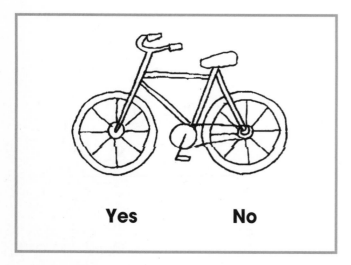

Yes   **No**

Yes   **No**

Tired Clown

Read the story and discuss what it means to feel tired. Then help the students cut and paste the pictures in the correct sentences.

Look at the clown.

The clown made the  laugh. Ha-Ha-Ha!

The clown made the  laugh. He-He-He!

The clown made the  laugh. Ho-Ho-Ho!

Now the clown feels  !

Name _____

Assessment

Read the story. Then help the students cut the character pictures and paste them next to the character's feeling.

Turtle sat by the pond. "I wish I had someone to play with," he said.

Along came Frog. "Hi, Turtle!" he said. "Guess what? I hopped over a lily pad. Then I hopped over two lily pads. Then I hopped over THREE lily pads!"

"Wow!" said Turtle. "Can you stay and play with me now?"

"No," said Frog. "I need to go tell the other animals. Bye!"

| | → | **lonely** |
| | | **proud** |

Overview Identifying Stated Main Idea

Directions and Sample Answers for Activity Pages

Day 1	See "Provide a Real-World Example" below.
Day 2	**Say:** *Many students wear backpacks to school. You can put books in a backpack. You can put pencils in a backpack. You can put papers in a backpack.* Discuss each sentence you stated and the picture that goes with it. Then help students color the picture that goes with the most important sentence, or main idea. (girl walking into a school wearing a backpack)
Day 3	Help the boys point to the words as they read the first line. Help the girls point to the words as they read the second line. Then read the third line. Discuss which sentence is the main idea. Ask students to color the speaker who stated the main idea. (teacher)
Day 4	Display several familiar nonfiction books. Ask students to choose one they like and draw a picture that could be in the book. As students share their pictures with the group, help them fill in the sentence. Then help them point to the words as they read their sentence to the group. **Say:** *(Student) stated a main idea. (He/She) said, "I like books about (topic)."*
Day 5	Help students cut out the pictures. Ask them to listen to the passage. Ask them to point to each word in the sentence below the passage as you read it together several times. Then ask students to glue on the picture that shows the main idea. (both flags) Afterward, meet individually with students to discuss their results. Use their responses to plan further instruction and review.

Provide a Real-World Example

◆ Hand out the Day 1 activity page. Help students cut out the pictures at the bottom of the page.

◆ **Say:** *My friend said, "I have many jars." I looked on her shelf. She had a jar of buttons. She had a jar of rocks. She had a jar of paper clips.*

◆ Help students locate the jars with buttons, rocks, and paper clips and glue them on the shelf.

◆ **Ask:** *What is the main, or most important, thing my friend said? Yes—she said, "I have many jars."* Write the word **jars** on the board. Then help students write the word on the line in the speech balloon and point to the words as they read the statement to a partner.

◆ Explain that we can also listen for the main idea when people read to us. Write the following on chart paper:

Stated Main Idea

Listen for the most important sentence.

Jars

**Read the story aloud. Help students cut and paste the correct items on the shelves.
Then ask them to finish the most important sentence below.**

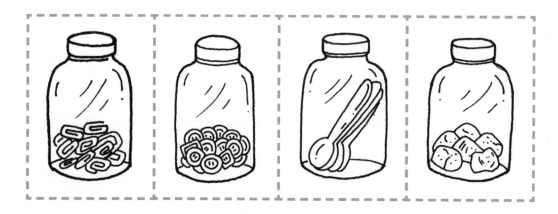

Backpacks

Read the story aloud and discuss the pictures. Help students color the picture that shows the main idea of the story.

Adding Apples

**Help the boys read the first line and the girls read the second line. Then read the third line.
Help the students color the speaker who read the main idea.**

 I have 1 .

 I have 2  .

 You have 3 in all.

A Book I Like

Ask the students to think about a book they like. Help them draw a picture from that book. Help them finish the sentence below.

I like books about _____.

Assessment

Read the story aloud. Help students cut the pictures below and paste the main idea in the box.

Look around!

You can see flags.

You can see a United States flag.

You can see stripes on the flag.

You can see a racing flag.

You can see squares on the flag.

You can see ⬜ .

Overview Identifying Supporting Details

Directions and Sample Answers for Activity Pages

Day 1	See "Provide a Real-World Example" below.
Day 2	Ask students to point to the words and read the main idea with you. Discuss the picture. Then help students color the items that are details about the beach. (umbrella, shovel, blanket, sand pail)
Day 3	Ask students to point to the words and read the main idea with you. Discuss the picture. **Say:** *The picture has no details to go with the main idea. Let's find some animals that could live on a farm. Could a cow live on a farm? Draw a circle around* **Yes** *or* **No**. Repeat with the other animals. (**Yes:** cow, pig, horse, chicken. **No:** giraffe, whale.)
Day 4	Divide the class into two groups of girls and two groups of boys. Read the first line. Help the first group of girls point to the words and read the second line. Help the first group of boys point to the words and read the third line. Help the second group of girls and boys read the fourth and fifth lines. **Say:** *The main idea is "Many people work in a community." Color the speakers who give supporting details. Then circle each supporting detail.* (**Girl 1:** doctor. **Boy 1:** construction worker. **Girl 2:** firefighter. **Boy 2:** chef.)
Day 5	Ask students to listen to the passage. Ask them to draw a circle around the picture that goes with the most important sentence. Then ask them to color the pictures that give more information about the main idea. Afterward, meet individually with students to discuss their results. Use their responses to plan further instruction and review. (**Main Idea:** insects. **Supporting Details:** dragonfly, ant, grasshopper, beetle.)

Provide a Real-World Example

◆ Hand out the Day 1 activity page.

◆ **Say:** *We have a nice class.* Point to this sentence on the page. Ask students to point to the words as they read this sentence with you.

◆ **Say:** *"We have a nice class" is a main idea. Now we will add some more information, or details, to this idea. Look around your table (or in your row). Who is in our nice class?* Allow time for students to Think/Pair/Share about some of the students who are in their class. Then ask them to draw three of the students in the boxes.

◆ Explain that we can also listen for details when people read to us. Add the following to the chart created the previous week:

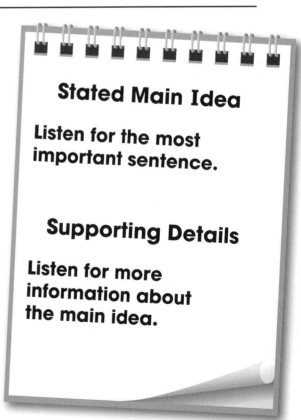

Stated Main Idea

Listen for the most important sentence.

Supporting Details

Listen for more information about the main idea.

Our Nice Class

Read the sentence. Then help students draw three of their classmates in the boxes below.

We have a nice class.

At the Beach

Read the sentence. Then ask students to color the things people bring to the beach.

People take things to the beach.

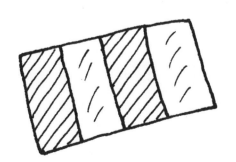  

On a Farm

Ask students whether each animal lives on a farm. Help them circle *yes* or *no* for each.

Many animals live on a farm.

Yes   No   **Yes   No**

Yes   No   **Yes   No**

Yes   No   **Yes   No**

Working in a Community

Read the story. Help students color the speakers who give supporting details.

Many people work in a community.

 A  works.

 A  works.

 A  works.

 A  works.

Assessment

**Read the passage. Ask students to circle the picture with the main idea.
Then ask them to color the pictures that show supporting details.**

Insects have 6 legs.

Ants have 6 legs.

Beetles have 6 legs.

Dragonflies have 6 legs.

Grasshoppers have 6 legs.

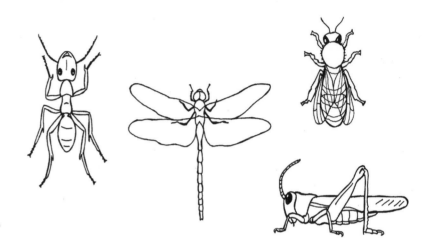

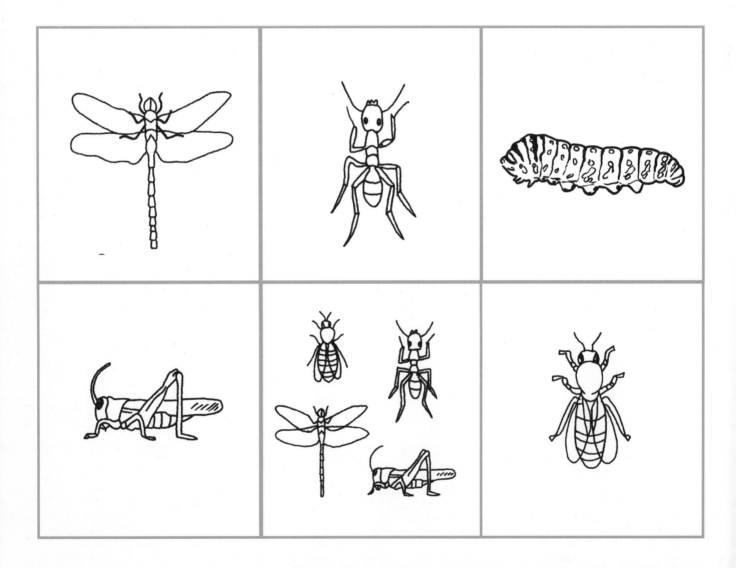

Overview Summarizing Fiction

Directions and Sample Answers for Activity Pages

Day 1	See "Provide a Real-World Example" below.
Day 2	**Say:** *Kim had a kite. The kite had a tail. The tail had ribbons on it. Kim flew her kite. She had fun.* Discuss the big ideas in the story. Then help students summarize the story and color the picture that goes with their summary. (Kim had fun flying a kite.)
Day 3	Help students cut out the pictures. **Say:** *Gus's dad drove him to the bus stop in his car. Gus rode the bus to Mrs. Kurt's house. Gus rode to the stables in Mrs. Kurt's truck. Now, Gus is riding a horse.* Help students choose the pictures that show the big ideas about Gus's day and glue them in the squares. Then ask them to point to the words in the circle and help you read the summary. (**Big Ideas:** horse, bus, car, truck.)
Day 4	Help students cut out the pictures. **Say:** *Bo is a big, spotted dog. One day, he found a bone. Bo was happy when he found the bone!* Next, ask students to point to the words as they read each big idea with you. Help them choose the correct picture to complete each big idea and glue it in place. Finally, help students summarize the story and draw a picture that goes with their summary. (**Big Ideas:** Bo is a dog. Bo has a bone. Bo is happy. **Summary:** A dog is happy because he found a bone.)
Day 5	As students listen to the story, ask them to draw a circle around each big idea beside the story box. When you finish, **say:** *Color the picture below that shows the best summary.* Afterward, meet individually with students to discuss their results. Use their responses to plan further instruction and review. (**Big Ideas:** girl, grandfather, 5 pennies, 1 nickel, 1 dime. **Summary:** A girl traded her coins for a dime.)

Provide a Real-World Example

◆ Hand out the Day 1 activity page.

◆ **Say:** *One day I had eggs for breakfast. One day I had cereal for breakfast. One day I had pancakes for breakfast. Draw a circle around the things I had for breakfast.*

◆ Allow time for students to circle the correct foods.

◆ **Say:** *I can tell about my breakfasts in one sentence:* **I like to eat different things for breakfast.** *This sentence is a summary. Do you like to eat different things for breakfast, too? Tell your partner what you like to eat.*

◆ Explain that we can also summarize stories we hear. Discuss a familiar story you have read to the class. Then ask students to help you tell about the story in one sentence. When you finish, write the following on chart paper:

Summarizing

Think about the most important parts.

Tell about the story in one sentence.

Name _____

Breakfast

Read the story. Ask students to circle the items mentioned in the story.

Unit 11 • Everyday Comprehension Intervention Activities Grade K • ©2010 Newmark Learning, LLC

Kim's Kite

Read the story aloud. Then help students color the picture that summarizes the story.

Gus on the Go

Read the story aloud. Then help the students cut and paste the pictures that summarize the story.

Bo

Read the story aloud. Then help the students cut and paste the pictures into the story. Help them draw a summary of the story below.

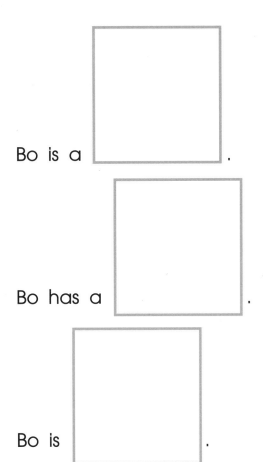

Bo is a _____ .

Bo has a _____ .

Bo is _____ .

Assessment

Read the story aloud and ask students to circle the big idea of each sentence. Then ask them to color the best summary.

"I have some coins," said Nan.

"Let's see what you have," said Grandpa.

Nan had five pennies. She had one nickel.

"I will trade you for a new coin," said Grandpa. Now Nan has a dime!

Overview Summarizing Nonfiction

Directions and Sample Answers for Activity Pages

Day 1	See "Provide a Real-World Example" below.
Day 2	**Say:** *Long ago, all firefighters were men. Today, women are firefighters, too. All firefighters wear special clothes, hats, boots, and gloves to stay safe.* Discuss the big ideas. Then help students summarize the information and color the picture that goes with their summary. (Some men and women are firefighters.)
Day 3	Help students cut out the pictures. **Say:** *An octopus is a sea animal. It has eight legs, called tentacles. A crab is a sea animal. It has eight legs, too. Some spiders live on water, and some live on land. A spider has eight legs.* Help students choose the pictures that show the big idea about the animals and glue them in the squares. Then ask them to point to the words in the circle and help you read the summary. (**Big Ideas:** octopus, crab, spider.)
Day 4	**Say:** *Get bread, peanut butter, and a knife. Spread the peanut butter on the bread. Put the bread together. Have a peanut butter sandwich to eat!* Next, ask students to point to the words as they read each big idea with you. Help them choose the correct picture to complete each big idea and glue it in place. Finally, help students summarize the story and draw a picture that goes with their summary. (**Big Ideas:** Get some bread. Get some peanut butter. Get a knife. **Summary:** You can have a peanut butter sandwich.)
Day 5	As students listen to the book review, ask them to draw a circle around each big idea beside the story box. When you finish, **say:** *Color the picture below that shows the best summary.* Afterward, meet individually with students to discuss their results. Use their responses to plan further instruction and review. (**Big Ideas:** book, cowboy hat, sun hat, tall top hat. **Summary:** Kids can read this book to learn about hats.)

Provide a Real-World Example

◆ Hand out the Day 1 activity page.

◆ **Say:** *I cleaned my house on Saturday morning. At nine o'clock, I dusted the furniture. At ten o'clock, I swept the floors. At eleven o'clock, I washed the windows. At twelve o'clock, I was done! Draw a circle around the things I did while I was cleaning my house.*

◆ Allow time for students to circle the correct tasks.

◆ **Say:** *I can tell about my cleaning in one sentence:* **I spent three hours cleaning my house on Saturday.** *This sentence is a summary. Do you clean your room? How long does it take? Tell your partner about cleaning your room.*

◆ Explain that we can also summarize information we learn about the world. Discuss a familiar science topic. Then ask students to help you tell about the topic in one sentence. When you finish, write the following on chart paper:

Summarizing

Think about the most important parts.

Tell about the information in one sentence.

Cleaning the House

Read the story aloud. Then ask students to circle the correct task for each hour.

  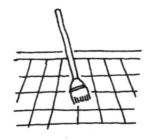 

Name _____

Firefighters

Read the story aloud. Ask students to color the picture that summarizes the story.

8 Legs

Read the story. Then help students cut out the pictures and paste the correct animals into the squares.

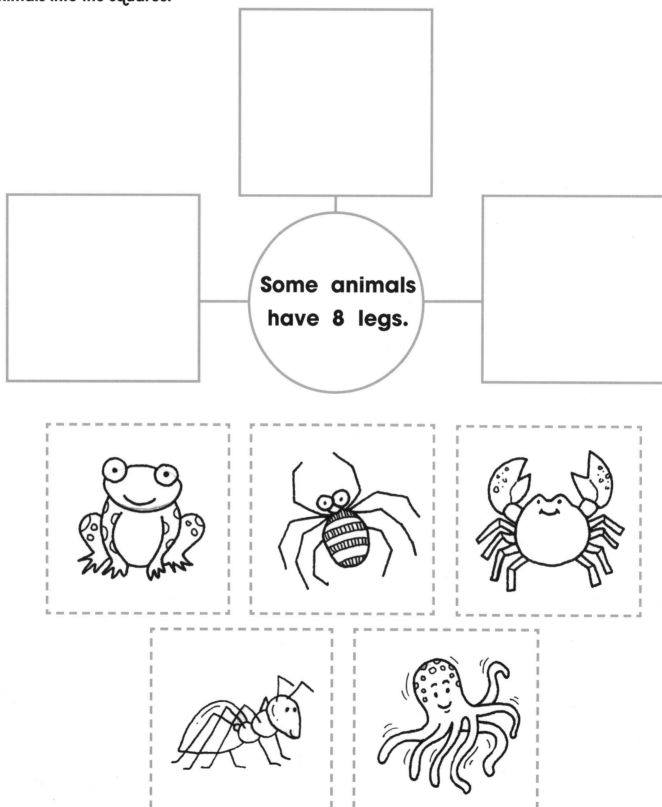

Some animals have 8 legs.

Peanut Butter Sandwich

Read the story. Then help students cut out and paste the pictures to complete each big idea.

Get some
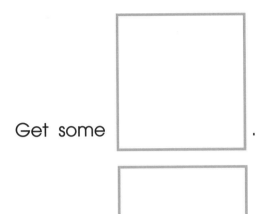
.

Get some
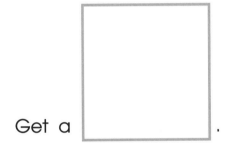
.

Get a
.

Help students draw a summary of the story.

Assessment

Read the story aloud. Ask students to circle each big idea. Then help students color the best summary.

I read a book called *Hats*.

I learned about cowboy hats.

I learned about sun hats.

I learned about tall top hats.

Would you like to learn about hats?

Read this book!

Overview Comparing and Contrasting in Fiction

Directions and Sample Answers for Activity Pages

Day 1	See "Provide a Real-World Example" below.
Day 2	**Say:** *Jay and Ray are twins. Jay and Ray want to dress alike. Color the hats that are alike.* Repeat the process with the T-shirts, jeans, and shoes. Then ask students to tell a partner how Jay and Ray are alike. (twins, same caps, same T-shirts, same jeans, same shoes)
Day 3	**Say:** *Zoe went to the park. She saw a fish in the pond. Then she saw another fish! Look at the pictures. Color the parts of the second picture that are different from the first picture. Then tell a partner how the second fish is different.* (it's not alive; it's part of a fountain; it's spouting water)
Day 4	**Say:** *Many stories have a queen and princess. Look at this queen and princess.* Discuss how the queen and princess are alike and different. Then help students mark the chart by placing an **X** in the appropriate column(s). (**Queen:** throne, scepter, crown, necklace. **Princess:** throne, crown, skirt, necklace.)
Day 5	Ask students to listen to the story. **Say:** *Point to number 1. Point to the blanket. Point to the quilt. Draw a circle around the one that Grandma made.* Repeat the procedure with number 2 (is soft) and 3 (will keep Ivy warm). Afterward, meet individually with students to discuss their results. Use their responses to plan further instruction and review. (**1:** quilt. **2:** blanket. **3:** quilt and blanket.)

Provide a Real-World Example

◆ Hand out the Day 1 activity page.

◆ Display a pencil and a crayon. **Say:** *We use pencils and crayons in our class. I can compare a pencil and crayon. I can tell how they are alike. They are alike because I can hold them in my hand. Draw a circle around the things you can hold in your hand.* Model how to draw a circle around the pencil and crayon beside the hand.

◆ Repeat the process with the other three rows. (**Comparing:** The pencil and crayon are alike because we can draw with them. **Contrasting:** The pencil is different because it is longer. The crayon is different because it is a color.)

◆ Explain that we can compare and contrast things in stories, too. Name two characters or settings from stories you have read to the class, and ask students to name ways they are alike and different. Then write the following on chart paper:

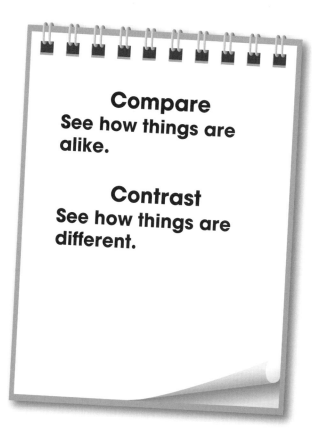

Compare
See how things are alike.

Contrast
See how things are different.

Pencil or Crayon?

Help students compare and contrast pencils and pens. Ask them to circle the correct item.

Ask students which one they can hold in their hands.

Ask students which one they can use to draw.

   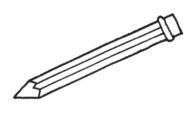   

Ask students which one is longer.

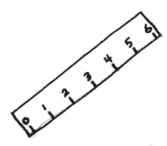      

Ask students which one they can use to color.

Jay and Ray

Ask students to color the items that are alike.

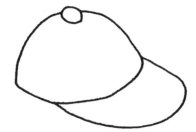 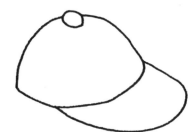 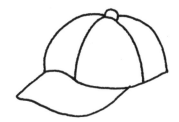

A Fishy Day

Help students color the parts of the second picture that are different from the first.

The Queen and the Princess

Ask students to compare and contrast the characters. Help them mark the correct boxes in the chart.

Assessment

Read the story aloud. Ask students to circle the correct items.

"I'm cold!" called Ivy.

Dad came running. He gave Ivy a blanket.

"This blanket will keep you warm. It's soft, too," said Dad.

Mom came running. She gave Ivy a quilt.

"Grandma made this quilt. It will keep you warm!" said Mom.

"Thank you!" said Ivy. "I'm not cold now!"

1. Ask students to circle what Grandma made.

2. Ask students to circle which is soft.

3. Ask students to circle which is warm.

Overview Comparing and Contrasting in Nonfiction

Directions and Sample Answers for Activity Pages

Day 1	See "Provide a Real-World Example" below.
Day 2	Point out Kansas on a United States map. **Say:** *The sunflower is the state flower of Kansas.* Help students color the petals of the flowers yellow, the centers brown, and the leaves and stems green. Then ask them to tell a partner how the two sunflowers are alike. (same size, same number of petals and leaves, same colors)
Day 3	**Say:** *People have beds. Look at these beds.* Discuss ways the beds are alike. (People sleep in them. They are in bedrooms.) Then **say:** *These beds are different, too. Different people sleep in them. Point to the top bed. Draw a line to show who sleeps in this bed.* Repeat with the middle and bottom beds. Then ask students to choose two of the beds and tell a partner another way they are different.
Day 4	**Say:** *People have many different types of clocks. Look at these clocks.* Discuss how the two clocks are alike and different. Then help students mark the chart by placing an **X** in the appropriate column(s). (**Wall Clock:** the number 7, clock hands, round. **Digital Clock:** the number 7, rectangular, a cord.)
Day 5	Ask students to listen to the passage. **Say:** *Point to number 1. Point to the house. Point to the houseboat. Draw a circle around the one that is on land.* Repeat the procedure with number 2 (has windows and doors) and 3 (is on water). Afterward, meet individually with students to discuss their results. Use their responses to plan further instruction and review. (**1:** house. **2:** house and houseboat. **3:** houseboat.)

Provide a Real-World Example

◆ Hand out the Day 1 activity page.

◆ Draw or display a glove and a mitten. **Say:** *Many people have gloves and mittens. I can compare gloves and mittens. I can tell how they are alike. They are alike because we wear them on our hands. Draw a circle around the things you can wear on your hands.* Model how to draw a circle around the gloves and mittens beside the hands.

◆ Repeat the process with the other three rows. (**Comparing:** Gloves and mittens are alike because people wear them on cold days. **Contrasting:** Gloves are different because they have separate fingers. Mittens are different because they are shaped like the state of Michigan. TIP: Point out Michigan on a United States map.)

◆ Explain that we can compare and contrast things that we learn about the world, too. Name two familiar animals, and ask students to name ways they are alike and different. Then write the following on chart paper:

Compare
See how things are alike.

Contrast
See how things are different.

Gloves or Mittens?

Read the passage. Ask students to circle the correct picture for each question.

Ask students which things we can wear on our hands.

Ask students which things keep our hands warm.

Ask students which things have separate fingers.

Ask students which things are shaped like Michigan.

Sunflowers

Help students color the sunflowers. Ask them to compare the flowers with a partner.

Beds

Ask students to match each bed with the person who sleeps in it.

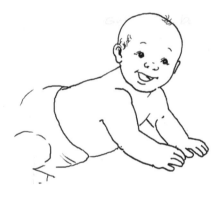

Clocks

Ask students to compare and contrast the clocks. Help them mark the appropriate boxes.

Assessment

Read the story aloud. Ask students to circle the correct items.

Some kids live in houses.

A house is on land.

A house has windows and doors.

Some kids live in houseboats.

A houseboat is on water.

A houseboat has windows and doors, too.

1. Ask students which home is on land.

2. Ask students which home has doors and windows.

3. Ask students which home is on water.

Unit 14 • Everyday Comprehension Intervention Activities Grade K • ©2010 Newmark Learning, LLC

Overview Identifying Cause and Effect in Fiction

Directions and Sample Answers for Activity Pages

Day 1	See "Provide a Real-World Example" below.
Day 2	Discuss the pictures. Then help students cut out the causes and glue them before the correct effects. (**First:** the yard needed raking/the boy raked. **Second:** the dog wanted to go out/the girl let him out.)
Day 3	**Say:** *Bea had too many baseball caps. What do you think happened? Draw a picture to show your idea.* Repeat the process with the mitts and bats. (Responses will vary but may include figuring out a place to store them or giving some of them away.)
Day 4	**Say:** *Liz likes rainy days. Sam doesn't like rainy days.* Discuss the pictures. Then ask the students to color each picture that shows something that could happen on a rainy day. (splashing in puddles, tracking in mud, having an indoor picnic, water in the birdbath)
Day 5	Help students cut out the pictures. Ask them to listen to the story. Then **ask:** *Which picture shows why something happened? Glue that picture in the first box. Which picture shows what happened? Clue that picture in the second box.* Afterward, meet individually with students to discuss their results. Use their responses to plan further instruction and review. (**Cause:** Ike wanted an apple and Grandpa wanted an apple pie. **Effect:** They went to the apple orchard.)

Provide a Real-World Example

◆ Hand out the Day 1 activity page.

◆ Ask the students to stand up. Ask them to sit back down. Then ask them to wave. **Say:** *Why did you stand up, sit down, and wave? Yes—you did these things because I asked you to. Together, we acted out a cause and effect. My request was the cause. Standing, sitting, and waving were the effects.*

◆ Ask students to draw a teacher asking the class to stand, sit, and wave. Then ask them to color each effect.

◆ Explain that we can also find causes and effects in pictures and stories. Write the following on chart paper:

Cause

Why did something happen?

Effect

What happened?

Teacher's Request

Ask students to draw a teacher making requests in the space. Then help them color the effects.

Please stand.
Please sit.
Please wave.

Helping Out

Help students cut out the pictures and paste them next to the correct effect.

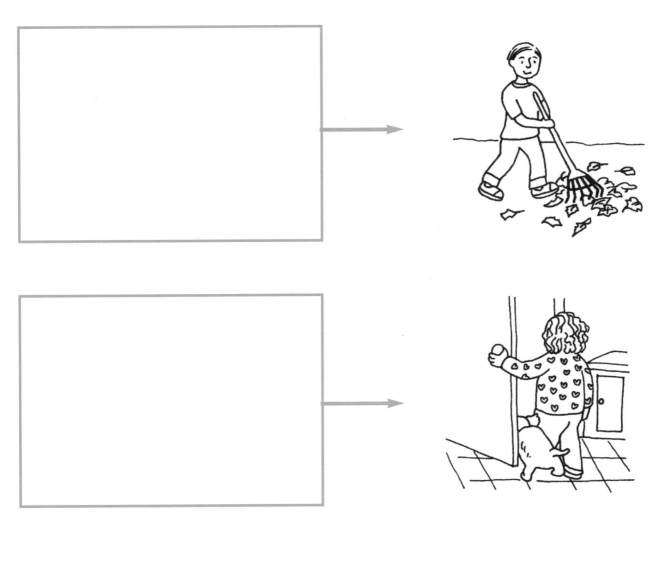

Bea Loves Baseball

Ask students to draw an effect for each cause.

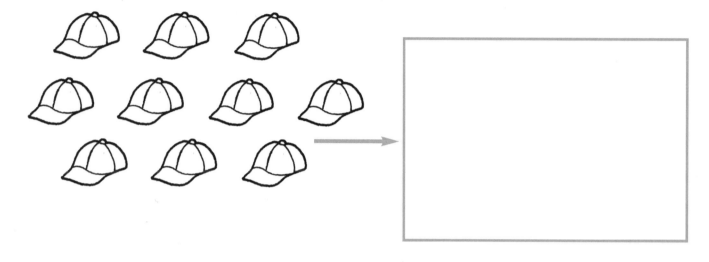

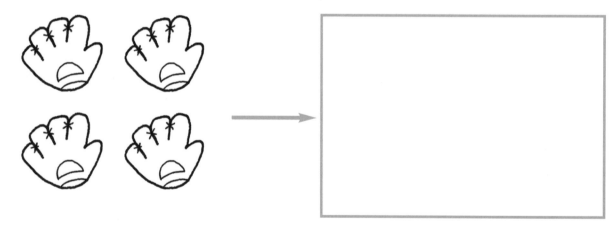

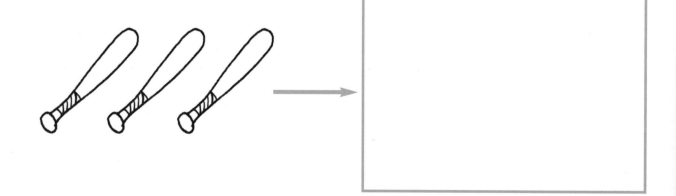

Rainy Day

Ask students to color the things that could happen on a rainy day.

Assessment

Help students cut out the pictures. Then ask them to paste the cause on the left and the effect on the right.

"I love apples," said Ike.

"I love apple pie," said Grandpa.

"Can we go to the store?" said Ike.

"Let's go to the orchard," said Grandpa.
"We can pick our own apples!"

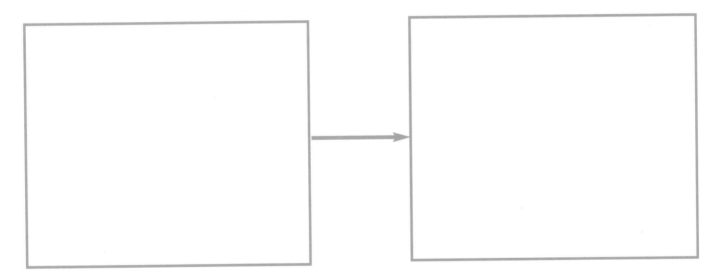

Overview Identifying Cause and Effect in Nonfiction

Directions and Sample Answers for Activity Pages

Day 1	See "Provide a Real-World Example" below.
Day 2	**Say:** *Many communities have parks. People like to go to the parks. Many things happen at a park.* Help students brainstorm things that could happen at a park. Discuss what causes each event to happen. Then help students draw one of the cause-and-effect relationships in the park picture. (going high on a swing because someone pushes you; feeding ducks in the pond because they are hungry; wearing a helmet so you will be safe on your bike; having a picnic because it's a beautiful day; leaving the flowers alone because the sign says not to pick them, etc.)
Day 3	**Say:** *Many people have gardens. Plants in a garden need water. Sometimes rain falls on the plants. Other times, people must put water on the plants.* Discuss the pictures. Then ask the students to color each picture that shows something that happens if a garden gets plenty of water. (healthy flowers in a garden, people eating garden vegetables, healthy vegetables in a garden, flowers in a vase)
Day 4	Help students cut out the shapes at the bottom of the page. Then help them fold each shape along the fold line. Discuss how the shapes change. **Say:** *Find the square at the top of the page. Folding the square causes it to turn into a new shape. Draw a line to the picture that shows what happens when you fold the square.* Repeat with the circle. (**Square:** rectangle. **Circle:** semicircle.)
Day 5	Help students cut out the pictures. Ask them to listen to the passage. Then **ask:** *Which picture shows why something happened? Glue that picture in the first box. Which picture shows what happened? Clue that picture in the second box.* Afterward, meet individually with students to discuss their results. Use their responses to plan further instruction and review. (**Cause:** People had to write letters or travel to talk. **Effect:** People invented telephones.)

Provide a Real-World Example

◆ Hand out the Day 1 activity page.

◆ **Say:** *Let's pretend we're having Red Day at school. Everyone is wearing a red T-shirt. Everyone is writing with a red pencil. Everyone is eating a red apple. A visitor comes. The visitor asks, "Why is everyone wearing a red T-shirt? Why is everyone writing with a red pencil? Why is everyone eating a red apple?" We tell the visitor the reason. "Because it's Red Day!" we say.*

◆ Ask students to draw a circle around the Red Day sign. **Say:** *Having Red Day is a cause, or why something happened.* Then ask them to color the T-shirt, pencil, and apple red. **Say:** *Red T-shirts, red pencils, and red apples are the effects. They are what happened on Red Day.*

◆ Explain that we can also find causes and effects in things we learn about the world. Write the following on chart paper:

Cause

Why did something happen?

Effect

What happened?

Red Day

Ask students to circle the Red Day sign. Then help them color the effects.

Parks

Help students draw some causes and their effects in the park.

Please do
not pick.

Watering the Garden

Ask students to color the things that can happen in a garden when it gets enough water.

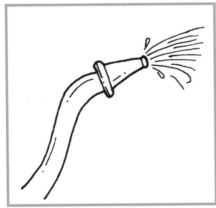

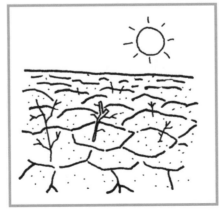

Folding Shapes

Help students cut out the shapes at the bottom of the page. Ask them to fold each shape on the fold line.

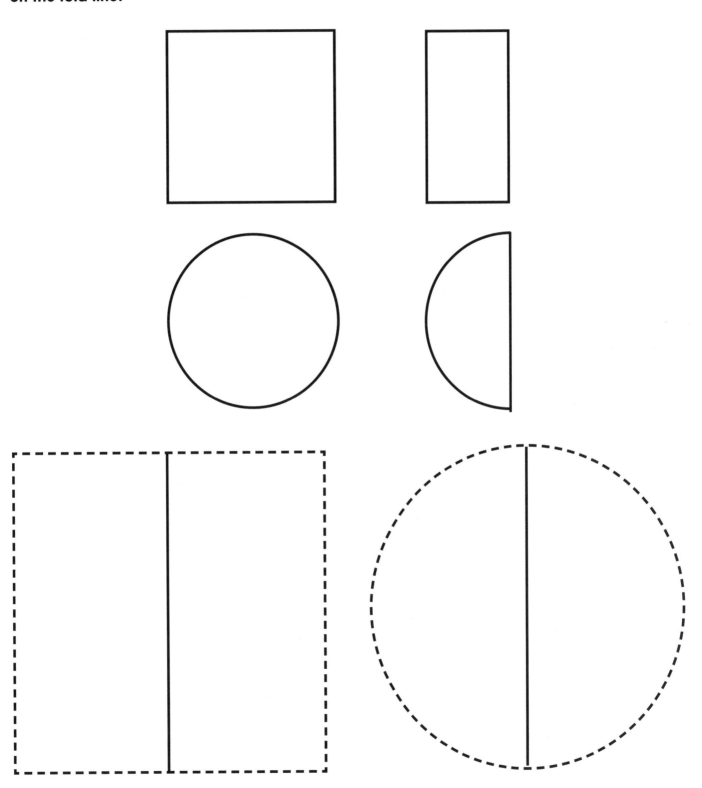

Assessment

Read the story. Then help students cut out the pictures. Ask them to paste the cause in the left box and the effect in the right box.

Long ago, people had no telephones.

People wrote letters to talk to one another.

People traveled to talk to one another.

People wanted a quicker way to talk.

So, people invented the telephone!

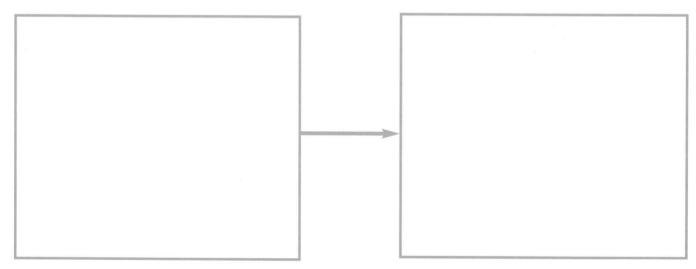

Overview Making Inferences in Fiction

Directions and Sample Answers for Activity Pages

Day 1	See "Provide a Real-World Example" below.
Day 2	**Say:** *Kip is going on a trip. What does Kip have?* (a sleeping bag) *The sleeping bag is a clue. What do you already know about sleeping bags?* (Responses will vary.) Help students use the clue and what they already know to infer where Kip will sleep tonight. Ask them to color the picture that shows their inference. (tent)
Day 3	**Say:** *Tom and Dee love to make things.* Discuss each set of supplies Tom and Dee use. **Say:** *The supplies are clues.* Ask students what they already know about each set of supplies. Then help them to make an inference about what Tom and Dee will make with each set of supplies. (Responses will vary but may include a poster or greeting card for the paper and markers, a decorated lunch sack or sack puppet for the sack and crayons, and a decorated sock or sock puppet for the sock and yarn.)
Day 4	**Say:** *Many stories are about friends. Look at the clues in each picture. Think about what you already know about friends.* Help students infer whether the people or animals in each picture are friends, then have them circle **Yes** or **No**. (**Yes:** cat/dog, kids on playground, girls cooking. **No:** fish, squirrels.)
Day 5	Ask students to listen to the story. **Say:** *Use the clues in the story and what you already know to figure out what Amy and Bud saw. Color the picture that shows what they saw.* Afterward, meet individually with students to discuss their results. Use their responses to plan further instruction and review. (twins in a stroller)

Provide a Real-World Example

◆ Hand out the Day 1 activity page.

◆ **Say:** *Lea is going to school. Going to school is a clue. I already know some things about school, too. I will look at the first row of pictures. I think Lea will wear the dress to school.* Ask students to color the dress.

◆ **Say:** *Now look at the next row. Remember, Lea is going to school. Think about what you already know about school. What will Lea take?* Discuss each item, and ask students to color the one Lea will take to school. (backpack)

◆ Explain that we can use clues and what we already know to help us figure out things in stories, too. Write the following on chart paper:

Making Inferences

Use clues.

Use what you already know.

Going to School

Ask students to circle what Lea will wear to school. Then ask them to circle what Lea will bring to school.

Kip's Trip

Ask students to circle where they think Kip will sleep tonight.

Making Things

Help students draw what they think Tom and Dee with make with each set of supplies.

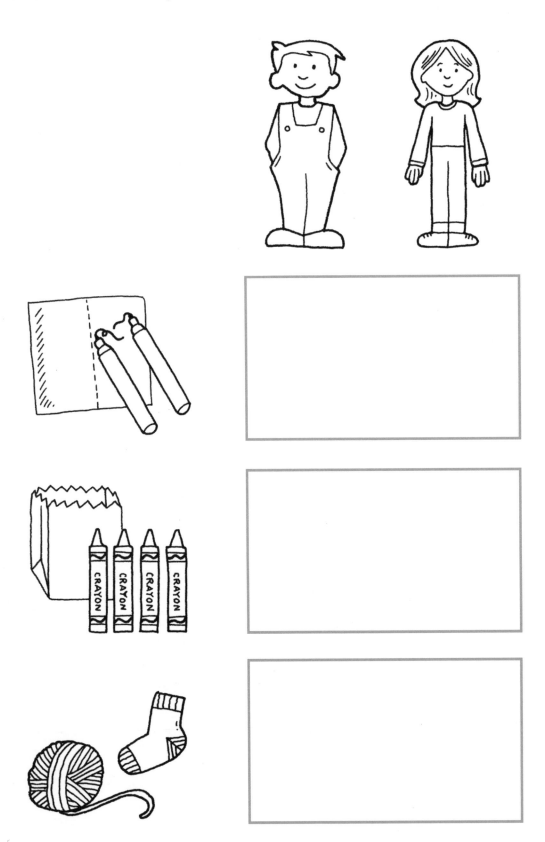

Name _____

Friends

Ask students whether each pair are friends. Help them circle *yes* or *no* for each.

Yes   No   Yes   No

Yes   No   Yes   No

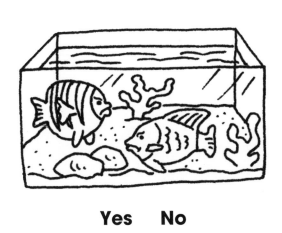

Yes   No

Assessment

Read the story aloud. Ask students to color what Amy and Bud saw.

Amy and Bud were at the lake. They were walking along the shore.

"It's fun seeing all the babies at the lake," said Amy.

"Yes," said Bud. "I saw some baby fish in the lake. I saw some baby birds in the tree, too."

"Look!" said Amy. "I see a dad taking some babies for a walk!"

"That's a fun way to go for a walk," said Bud.

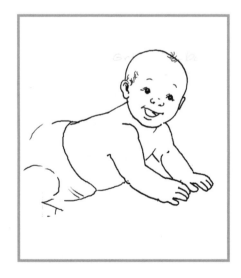

Overview Making Inferences in Nonfiction

Directions and Sample Answers for Activity Pages

Day 1	See "Provide a Real-World Example" below.
Day 2	**Say:** *Doctors have signs outside their offices. Look at Dr. Kim's sign. What does the sign look like?* (a toothbrush) *The shape of the sign is evidence. What do you already know about toothbrushes?* (Responses will vary.) Help students use the evidence and what they already know to infer what kind of office Dr. Kim has. Ask them to color the picture that shows their inference. (dentist's office)
Day 3	**Say:** *People often eat different foods for breakfast, lunch, and dinner. The food on the plates is evidence.* Ask students what they already know about each type of food. Invite them to point to the words in the right column as you read them. Then help them to make an inference about which meal each plate is for and draw a line to the correct word. (**Sandwich and Apple:** Lunch. **Meat and Peas:** Dinner. **Eggs and Bacon:** Breakfast.)
Day 4	**Say:** *People use tools in their jobs. Builders have many tools in their toolboxes. Look at the evidence in each picture. Think about what you already know about builders.* Help students infer whether the tool in each picture goes in a builder's toolbox and circle **Yes** or **No**. (**Yes:** hammer, saw, screwdriver, measuring tape. **No:** needle and thread, blender.)
Day 5	Ask students to listen to the letter. **Say:** *Use the evidence in the letter and what you already know to figure out what Grandma gave Kay for her birthday. Color the picture that shows what Kay got.* Afterward, meet individually with students to discuss their results. Use their responses to plan further instruction and review. (baseball and bat)

Provide a Real-World Example

◆ Hand out the Day 1 activity page.

◆ **Say:** *Nate made some cupcakes. Then some friends came over. The cupcakes and friends are evidence. You know something about cupcakes and friends, too. Think about the evidence and what you already know. What will Nate do?* Discuss each idea and ask students to color the one that shows what Nate will do. (share the cupcakes with his friends)

◆ Explain that we can use evidence and what we already know to help us figure out things in the world, too. Write the following on chart paper:

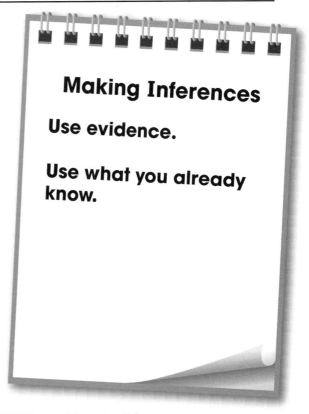

Making Inferences

Use evidence.

Use what you already know.

Cupcakes

Ask students to color the picture that shows what Nate will do.

Signs

Ask students to color the picture that shows what kind of office Dr. Kim has.

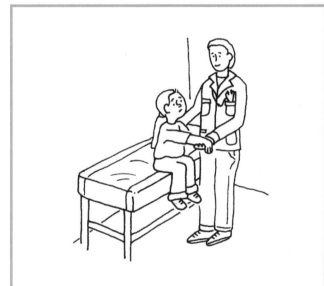

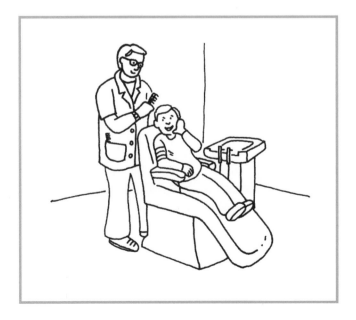

Name _____

Breakfast, Lunch, and Dinner

Help students match the food with the correct meal.

Breakfast

Lunch

Dinner

Tools

Ask students which tools go in a builder's toolbox. Help them circle *yes* or *no* for each item.

Yes   No   Yes   No

Yes   No   Yes   No

Yes   No   Yes   No

Assessment

Help students color the picture that shows what Kay got.

Dear Grandma,

    Thank you for the birthday present. I played with it every day this week. Today is rainy, though. So I played with something else.

I will come visit you soon!

Love,

Kay